A CENTURY
OF STORIES
NEW HANOVER COUNTY PUBLIC LIBRARY
1906-2006

WILD WILD WORLD

DRAGONFLIES

by Liza Jacobs

BLACKBIRCH®
PRESS

THOMSON
✳
GALE

San Diego • Detroit • New York • San Francisco • Cleveland • New Haven, Conn. • Waterville, Maine • London • Munich

© 2003 by Blackbirch Press™. Blackbirch Press™ is an imprint of The Gale Group, Inc., a division of Thomson Learning, Inc.

Blackbirch Press™ and Thomson Learning™ are trademarks used herein under license.

For more information, contact
The Gale Group, Inc.
27500 Drake Rd.
Farmington Hills, MI 48331-3535
Or you can visit our Internet site at http://www.gale.com

Photographs © 1996 by Wen-Kuei

Cover photograph © Corbis

© 1996 by Chin-Chin Publications Ltd.

No. 274-1, Sec.1 Ho-Ping E. Rd., Taipei, Taiwan, R.O.C.
Tel: 886-2-2363-3486 Fax: 886-2-2363-6081

LIBRARY OF CONGRESS CATALOGING-IN-PUBLICATION DATA

Jacobs, Liza.
  Dragonflies / by Liza Jacobs.
    v. cm. -- (Wild wild world)
  Includes bibliographical references.
  Contents: About dragonflies -- Expert fliers -- Eating and being eaten
-- Many sizes and colors.
   ISBN 1-4103-0042-0 (hardback : alk. paper)
   1. Dragonflies--Juvenile literature. [1. Dragonflies.] I. Title. II. Series.

  QL520.J23 2003
  595.7'33--dc21

                                                                2003001466

Printed in Taiwan
10 9 8 7 6 5 4 3 2 1

Table of Contents

About Dragonflies

Dragonflies and damselflies are so closely related that damselflies are often called dragonflies, too. An adult dragonfly is a beautiful sight. Like other insects, the body of a dragonfly has three main parts. It has a head, a thorax (midsection), and an abdomen (rear section).

Dragonflies have short antennae and large, curved compound eyes on their head. A dragonfly's compound eyes are made up of thousands of tiny eyes. Dragonflies can see in many directions at once and have amazing eyesight!

A dragonfly's thorax is big and strong. Its 2 pairs of wings and 3 pairs of legs are attached to the thorax. A dragonfly has large lacy wings. Its legs are spiny and each one has a little hook at the end for grasping things.

A dragonfly's abdomen is long and thin. The end of a male's abdomen is designed for holding on to a female during mating. Females have a sharp tip at the end of their abdomen.

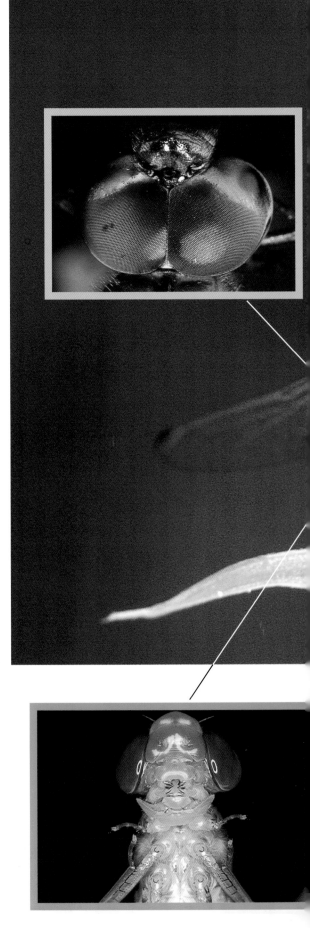

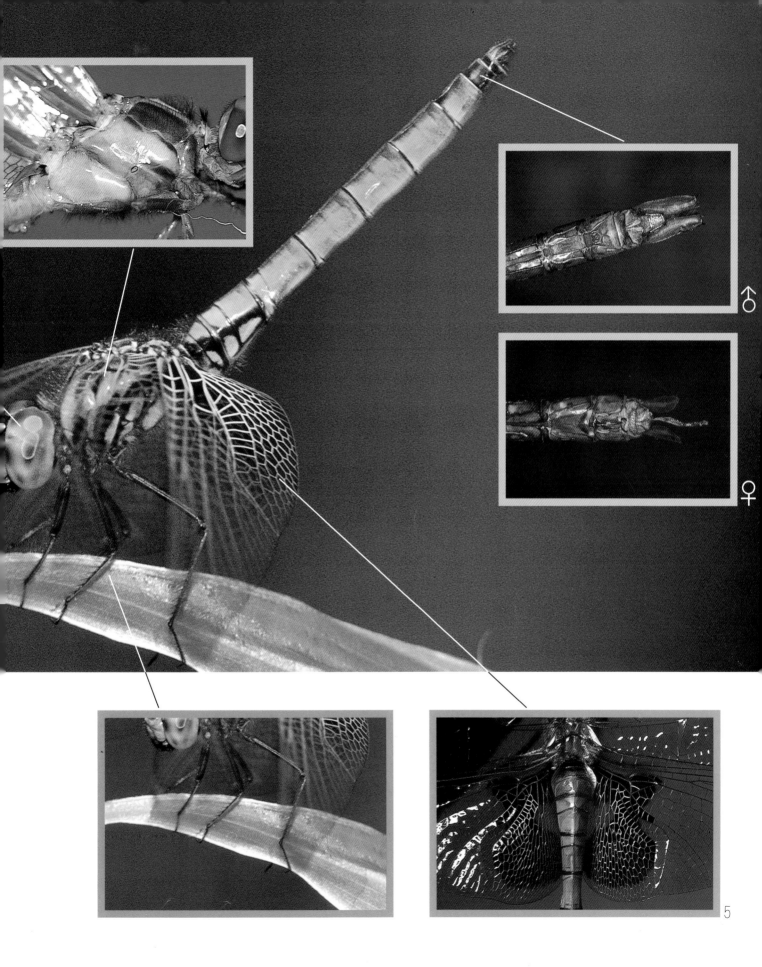

♂

♀

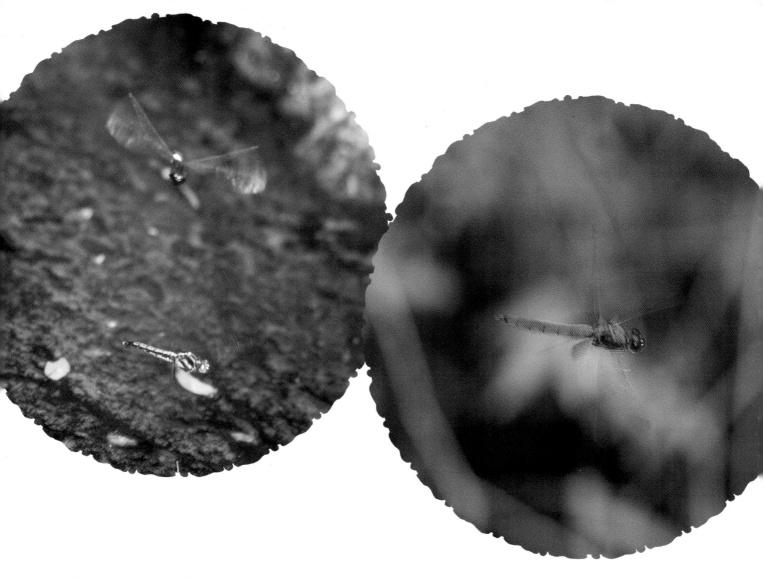

Expert Fliers

Dragonflies are expert fliers. Unlike many insects with two pairs of wings, a dragonfly is able to move each pair of wings separately. This gives a dragonfly extra speed and the ability to twist and turn smoothly in the air. They are strong fliers that can fly as fast as 30 miles per hour!

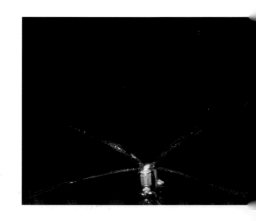

Eating and Being Eaten

Dragonflies are excellent hunters. Their keen eyesight helps them spot their next meal up to 40 feet away! And they are swift enough to be able to snatch up bees, flies, mosquitoes, butterflies, and other kinds of insects with their legs as they fly through the air!

Dragonflies also have to be on the lookout for creatures that want to eat them! Frogs eat dragonflies. So do spiders, birds, snakes, and other insects.

Cleaning

After dragonflies eat, they carefully clean themselves. They often find a quiet resting spot on a branch, leaf, or rock.

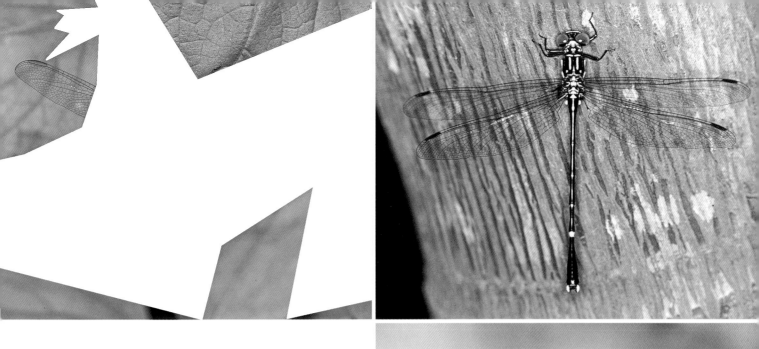

Then they use the little brushes on their front legs to clean all over their face.

Mating

To mate, a male dragonfly holds onto a female's head with the tip of his abdomen. Then the female bends her abdomen up toward him so they form a loop.

After mating, some female dragonflies dip their abdomen into the water to lay their eggs. Others use the sharp end of their abdomen to poke tiny egg holes into a leaf or stem near the water.

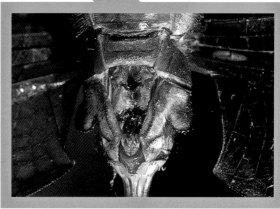

Generally,
dragonfly eggs
are round and
damselfly
eggs look like
little tubes.

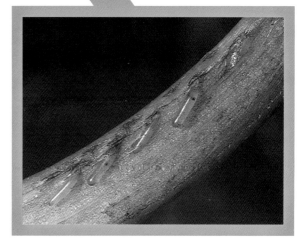

Three Stages of Growth

Dragonflies go through three stages of life as they grow into adults. The first stage is the egg. Then a baby, or nymph, hatches from the egg. Most of this second stage is lived underwater. Unlike adults, nymphs do not have fully formed wings and they breathe with gills.

Nymphs are fierce hunters and eat all kinds of small water animals. They have a special lip that stays folded up under their head when not in use. Then, when a nymph goes after a meal, it shoots out a lip half the length of its body!

As nymphs grow, they shed their outer covering several times. This is called molting. A newer, larger covering is underneath. When a nymph has grown as much as it can, it is ready for the third stage of life—changing into an adult. At nightfall the nymph climbs out of the water for the first time.

Out of the Old Skin

What happens next is amazing! A nymph finds a good spot on a rock or stem and waits for a few hours while its skin begins to dry out. When it is dry, the skin splits down the back. The dragonfly spends the next few hours slowly wriggling and pulling itself, headfirst, out of its old skin.

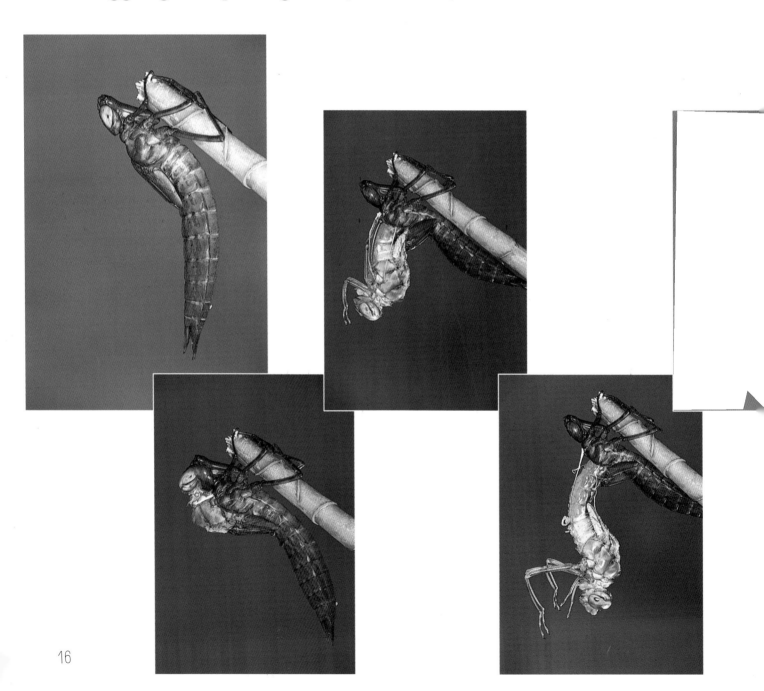

It then turns itself around and grabs onto the dead skin to rest. Slowly, its wings dry and are stretched out. By morning, an adult dragonfly is ready to fly off, find a mate, and begin the life cycle all over again!

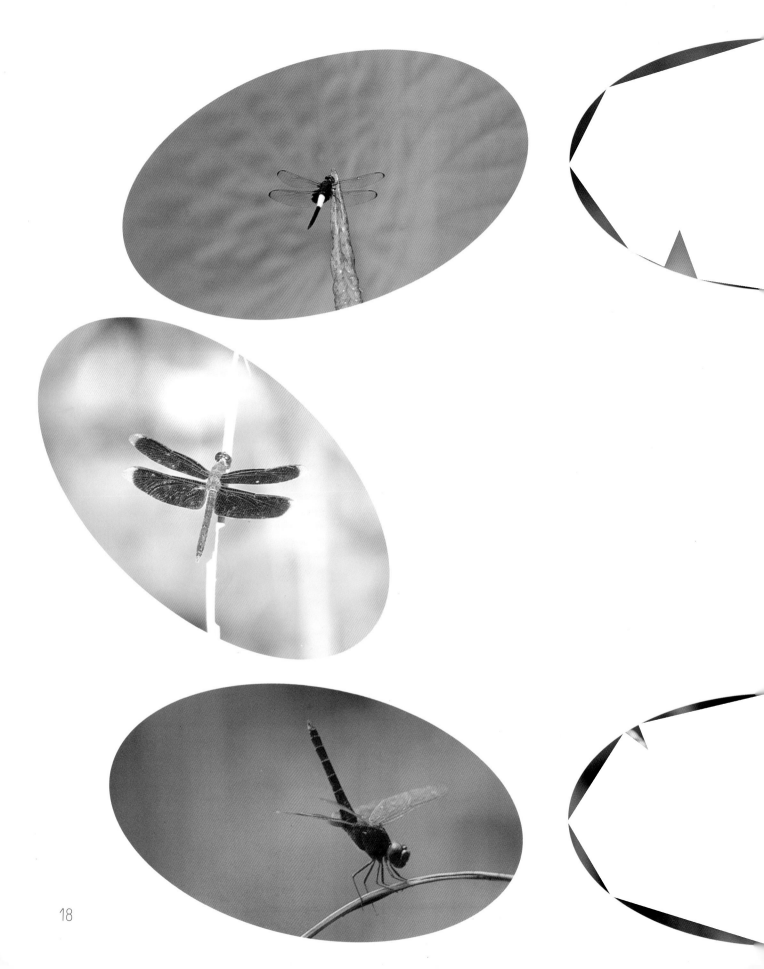

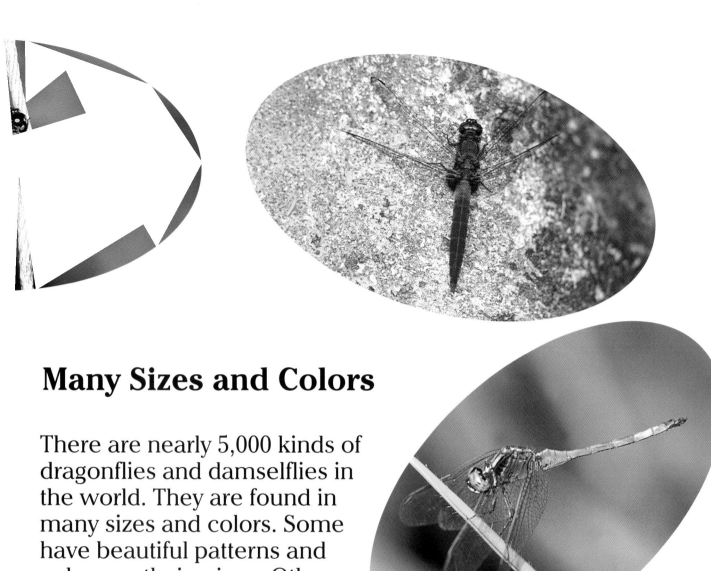

Many Sizes and Colors

There are nearly 5,000 kinds of dragonflies and damselflies in the world. They are found in many sizes and colors. Some have beautiful patterns and colors on their wings. Others have brightly colored or patterned abdomens.

① ② ③ ④ ⑤ ⑥

Damselflies and Dragonflies

Dragonflies and damselflies are very closely related and go through the same stages of life. One way to tell them apart is by the position of their wings while resting. Dragonflies usually hold their wings out flat.

Damselflies often fold the front pair upright. Damselflies have longer, thinner abdomens than dragonflies. Also, a damselfly's eyes bulge out on either side of its head. And damselflies often sit on a leaf and eat, while dragonflies eat in the air.

These close-ups show some of the differences between dragonflies and damselflies.

Dragonflies

Dragonflies rest with their wings spread out.
Damselflies rest with their wings folded upright.

Dragonflies have thicker abdomens than damselflies.

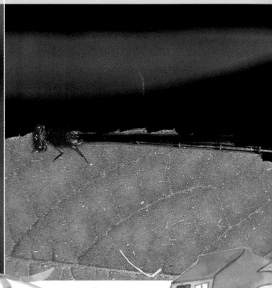

Damselflies

Dragonfly nymphs have gills tucked
inside their abdomens.
Damselfly nymphs have three
feathery gills on the outside.

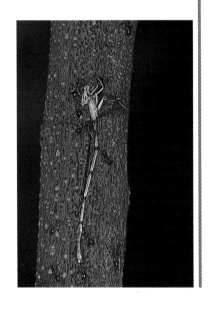

For More Information

St. Pierre, Stephanie. *Dragonflies*. Crystal
Lake, IL: Heinemann Library, 2001.

McEvey, Shane F. *Dragonflies*. Broomall,
PA: Chelsea House, 2001.

Meister, Cari. *Dragonflies*. Edina, MN:
ABDO Publishing, 2002.

Glossary

compound eye an eye that has many lenses

molt to shed the outer covering

nymph the second stage in a dragonfly's life

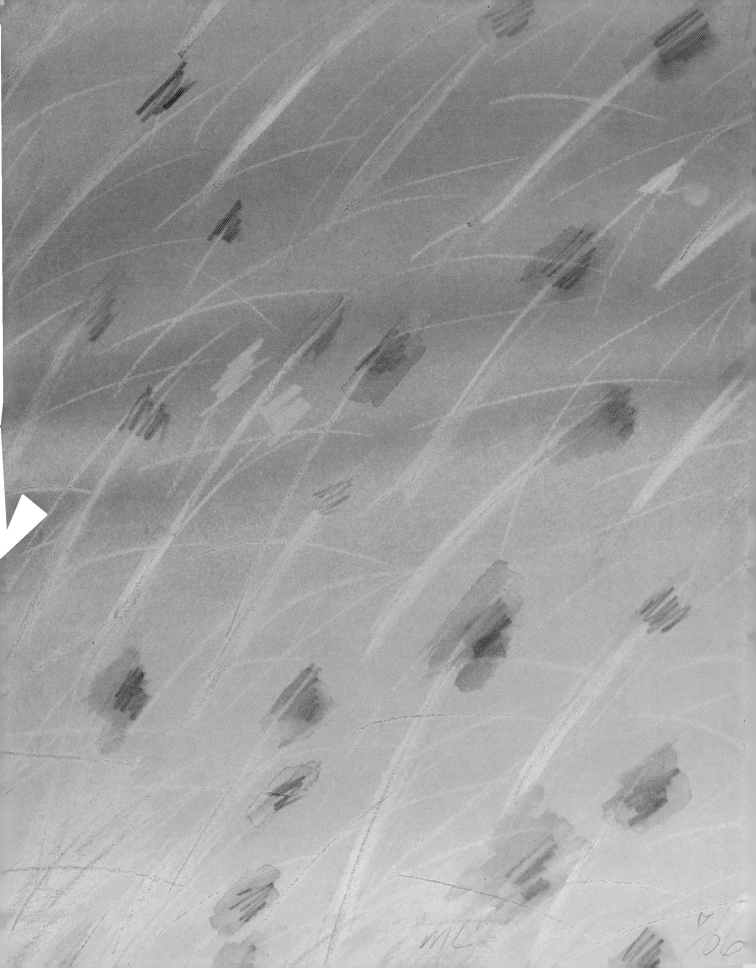